OXFORD
UNIVERSITY PRESS

Grandad and Me

Chantelle Greenhills

Here I am with my grandad.
We are good friends.

When my grandad was my age things were very different.

3

Here is my grandad. He is at school.
This is his class photo.

GREENHITHE
SCHOOL
ROOM 4 YEAR 1

Here I am at school. This is my
class photo.

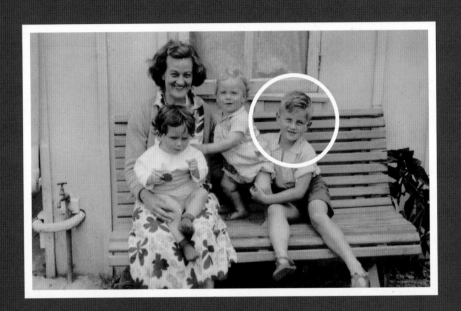

Here is my grandad outside his house.
His house is made of wood.

Here I am. I am outside my house.
My house is made of bricks.

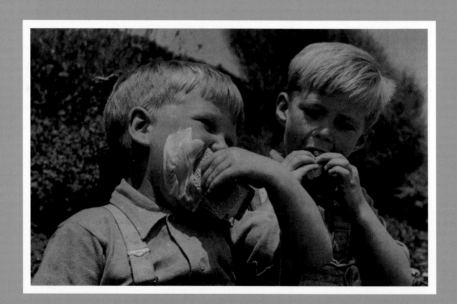

My grandad is eating an ice cream.
It is white ice cream in a wafer.

I am eating an ice cream. My ice cream is brown, orange and green. It is in a cone.

My grandad is playing with a toy. It is a sailing boat and it is his favourite toy.

I am playing with my favourite toy. It is a computer game.

My grandad is playing cricket. He is batting. His brother is the wicket keeper.

I am playing cricket. I am batting
and my mum is bowling.

Here is my grandad. He is standing beside his father's car. It is a Morris Isis.

Here I am standing beside my father's car. It is a four-wheel drive car.

Grandad

Me